art cure

un-alone in poetry

Mario Gabriel Adame

Library of Congress Control Number (LCCN):
2016905601

Print Book Edition
ISBN: 0692664602
ISBN-13: 978-0692664605

Published in the United States by
Dead Poets Dream Publishing
San Antonio, TX

To those children we worked with who have suffered abuse and neglect, I pray you never lose your voice. Your spirit does not leave my heart, and I hope during your roughest days, you do not give up on finding a peaceful way to cope.

To my dad who underwent a bone marrow transplant, we are blessed for having you with us in 2016. To my tío Israel who donated his platelets, our family appreciates you. And mom, you are one strong woman for standing by dad throughout his deepest fears, while tending to each of our family needs, including your first grandbaby.

acknowledgement

Throughout my life, I had been unable to discover ways for intuitively surrendering every part of my healthy well-being to one person. This chaotic struggle did not make it possible for me to fully trust myself or any other thing around me. Maybe, I became cynical from parental infidelity and having known the direct political implications of how a military family could be devastated with lifelong scars. Maybe, I found people less interested in maintaining undeniable intentions of his or her loyalty towards eternally loving any one thing, or any one person. So in turn, I strongly felt I did not know what absolute trust looked like between two people, nor did I claim witness to a person who persistently sacrificed everything for one purpose.

Despite actively learning how to become a genuine and productive citizen in both the digital age of rising social network's instant profiles and the post-*9/11* America of frequently contesting morals on terrorism and religion, I knew I had sustained an everyday visualization for proving loyalty and peace between two entities did not totally die; that perseverance of loyalty above all human traits would always survive to be a permanent gauge to balance love's physiological equation.

Mercifully, she came along. One gasp at a time, my temperament started the honest process for cleansing resentment. She kept passion and inspiration alive, when flashbacks of my life crushed me, and I found myself barely breathing for air from inability to recognize such patience and calmness in my soul. She knew exactly where to shine a light of gentleness, and with such glow, her loyalty helped expose what my faith required to experience its actual completion.

She was the strangest, but with each poem and prose written by her that she shared, I read, and fittingly she became a part of me. Though we had different childhood experiences, we happened to latch onto one another at a sensual peak of our adulthood. Each time I saw her, I felt words peeling from her skin. I envisioned letter-by-letter crawling slowly, moving in and out her bloodstream as a bubble, like those embedded inside a tubular spirit level. Each bubble represented a moment in time of her past that caught up to me. Yet, if she never said a word, but projected with her eyes those moments against the will of this face, I would feel her skin to understand the time capsule of true emotion. Her unspoken words channeled deep flow within my mind. So, as I recited them, I found cadence, and it led me to follow her body design into a place where our feelings connected in silence.

She empowered my hands through physical touch and by written language. This combination taught me to never forget how beneficial a certain calm and patience can be when two severed bodies need to begin integration for healing. What her silence gave then became surviving qualities today, and the most significant virtue continuing here with me is her bravery. Whichever ways a higher power allowed our universe to exactly align, I am stronger for a mutual path shared with her. Further, I am thankful for how she reinforced human spirit characteristics that I had been blessed with.

Together we became more un-alone.

The following poems and prose pieces I authored are built with lines entailing: forgiveness for my temper's negative tendencies, an internal self-transformation led by the remarkable children we served in our line of civic engagement, her poetic physical nature and its brave language equilibrium entering my soul's inhabitancy, and the escape to recover a cure for renewing each of our spiritual convictions.

It should be noted for the titles and themes in this book's assortment, each are ordered relative to a mode in which an intense sensation replays back from my mind to my body.

An 'Image' is that which presents an intellectual and emotional complex in an instant of time.

It is the presentation of such a "complex" instantaneously which gives that sense of sudden liberation; that sense of freedom from time limits and space limits; that sense of sudden growth, which we experience in the presence of the greatest works of art.

- Ezra Pound

Contents

art cure

un-alone in poetry

prelude to empire nights

Reaching for a couch limb,
  each vertebra laid on area rug
  next to the brink of frame railing;
and the other hand
  frantic without sensation,
  pushing down on tiled floor;
what I look for
  blood pump protrudes minimal light,
  where instant passions
  has unconsciously written
  on steno pad
  with explicit photograph.

new age P.T.S.D.
(new age Poetry Tattoos Saving Dignity)

His modern day
           misbehave,
        ideogrammic selling *Ezra*
by the raw heart pound,
          laced
in ways begging for moods of pure ecstasy.
They all extraordinary sculpted nightly *Frost*,
        anticipating details in the fabric,
        like *Jason Mraz* song for the lost.

They called him *the playground child,*
        in jungle gyms
        around a tatted poetry palace.
Roses pulled and in these two hands,
        sneakin' ways naturally come numb
        to replant the friend climb,
from ungodly work dates, and
learning novel ink of international queens
        on their *MacBook* word plates.

spotless feelings

You put pressure on this smile,
     when
tender kisses cannot repeat one more denial.

Maybe, folks say I'm like the others,
     but I can guarantee
I'll forever make your heart beat
     like there is nothing left to wonder!

What do you say to that?
     Don't give me your back.

You evaporate bleeding
from my open scars,
filled them
     to unleash intolerable parts
          of one heart.
Letter-by-letter
releasing from one another
led like oxygen's untangle,
surrender I do to you
at every 360° angle.

I don't want to be the same.
I don't want to be a light bulb to change.

I need perennial love.
I'm telling you,
        you're only as good
        as the company you keep.

Is this the place caging all your decisions?

Where are your exes?

Ready to try something different?

No?
It seems
        when we mix *past*
        and *future* moments,
        our emotions manufacture crutches.

I'm here.
        Yes, I can be extreme;
                oh, and a little too much?

Look,
        my love is *present*,
                so stable
        when you're unwell, and unable.

Distance
        is the persistence
                        of patient healing,
when your heart goes on vacation,
        or
when it puts in work,
        some how,
I am still here
        to remember what you are worth.

I am here to clean up the mess,
        that I *live* when you *leave*.
I continue to give when you are fearful,
and too confused to let your mind receive.

I scream for you!
        Spotless feelings,
                I have for you!

I don't

It was a good morning
    in the mirror,
    until
you see a face,
    fading,
        fleeing,
            worlds flipping.
I walk down the street,
wondering if you're in the same sheet,
    with him,
        in his car,
            in his apartment,
    while my heart is lament.

You cut me up,
    chained me one too many times,
left me stray at the hands of God's sewn;
    You bred this soul to fill its stone.

    oh no more! oh no more!
    I don't! I don't!

I wrote, *now* reading,
choking on my words;
      marry me!
      love me!
      let me die in your arms!

Buried two smiles
      among yesterday's mum voices.

What is love when there's more than one?
What is love when you're okay with gone?

I screamed, *I'm still here!*
Stripped,
      naked,
            completely humiliated,
roses dripping petal
      by petal.

Time is me knowing
      your better human being!
I demanded
      come out your missing dignity!

You cut me up,

       chained me one too many times,

left me stray at the hands of God's sewn;

       You bred this soul to fill its stone.

       oh no more! oh no more!

       I don't! I don't!

What did I have to do?

I played for keeps.

I needed you for the rest of life.

I wanted you to fight.

Why couldn't you be proud of me

       for loving every moment

              I couldn't see,

              I resurrected in we.

              I wouldn't give up!

Babe, my true love,

whenever I shall meet you,

I believe

       you are not truly waking up,

       if it is with any other man

       but loyal me!

the moans we share

The moans we share
      don't compare
            to hushed beat screams
      going off inside this airtight cavity,
            rooted deep down
      where *Never* sleeps,
            clicking and *inviting*
      to find its more perfect extremes.

Before I started writing in the dark,
unexpectedly,
      we painted a body spark.
Her light, light blue iris glow,
      then, my gimme brown ray,
us creating our own immediate grave.
Or will we climax making love 'til we are grey?
Miss Eyes, I'm passed need to behave.

When *you*
say my name with your tongue roll,
      I am under your body rule.

She had me
something in-between
I can only begin to describe.

Her ocean wave thrust upon my heart,
      hit eye to eye,
stimulation fantasy turned real;
      back and forth marathon sport,
an urgency holding me in her sweetest court.

Her second hand continues unwind,
      back in time,
to invent another moment,
      here through my boundless rhyme.

Mystic hands
      feeling every edge,
      like wrinkle finger tips,
        mine, hers,
and there my guns go, go, go
beyond friendly triggers.
      More arsenal
slashing swifter than a hundred daggers.

Baby, open up your portal,
fuck everything,
       but *please* don't *fuck* me twice,
'cause this thinnest blanket underneath
       will lead
       to *me* drowning inside electricity
       colder than your twitchin' skin ice.

Am I not asking for this love tonight?
One more time!
Gimme warmth, *Miss Amori*,
in body-knocking two souls' charm right.

slip

Is the slip, coming

         on

   and

         off

   your body

     gently,

a metaphor in how you keep

   your soul's curtain for

     a chase,

         a scream,

     a pain,

         a breath,

    a step,

         a smile

    a dance,

         a laugh.

A scene *by* scene

         history,

    just to *ask me*,

           just to *show me*,

how you want me?

love drop

As my eyes dissect your body's edges,
I envision *the art of exclamation marks,*
      that cannot neglect
      frames' mix of confetti and ashes.
My heart is beating hysterically,
      like twenty-six miles ran.
The chest skin and bone mineral prepares its
residence for soul pulsate before you and I,
while my right hand urges to retrace
      the softness of your left hip and thigh.
Next, my left hand on your right side,
        undertaking the high.
I can't help but firmly kiss once,
        then, long sigh.
      Chest-to-chest perspire one,
        what is yours and mine.
Babe, your emotion is needed, like
      love
        drop,
          drips this sweat
      beggin' to regain electrolyte.

The Darkest Tree

Have you seen the children
        who wait for one last leaf
                to fall from the tree?

There were actually three.
Three kinders watched as I drew this tree.
They didn't know what it would be,
        'til they took time to see.
They put down their crayons
        and saw rising branches,
as each began to take their shapes.

I told those three kinders,
  "This is *The Darkest Tree*,"
like the oak tree living outside my house.
I asked, *"How does it feel to be the tree?"*
   and
"How does it feel to be the only leaf?"

I thought I could use this idea, maybe to
help with name-calling, sharing, seasons
changing, and what comes with healing.

Knowing each one will lose the other,
   and the one who will lose more,
I didn't speak out loud any further,
   for this comforted me in my nurture.

I continued a talk in my mind:

The lightest thing know to gravity,
how the leaf will fall on earth;
its most silent tragedy.
Slowly, when the leaf falls, it will decay
and possibly have one more day
to move by the life of wind.

Or it becomes scooped up in a bag
amongst the rest of what was once dangling.
The tree remains cold
and waits for new season to begin
just to have more leaves again.

When you laid your full body
          on me,
and we began to sleep,
I woke up to a sight of your soft hair
and forehead, your eyes closed,
with a calmest sound of you sleeping.
I wondered if you were dreaming.

For a second or two,
the moment belonged to nature.
I didn't know how I fell asleep, but
inside our sleep and at my wake,
I was the freest.
I breathed just to breathe in;
I didn't breathe to catch air
away from my anxiety.
I was the luckiest
for it all having found us;

only you and me.

For a second or two,
I was the lightest thing know to gravity.
      We were.
But now that you are not here,
      I am the tree.
Gone is our love,
        like

            the

                last

                    leaf.

near

is it me?
      is it you?
disappearing
      like a spray of perfume

magic comes,
      contagion separates
bodies
      laying
         and
            clearing
      like wildfire smoke resonates

skin hold on tight

In the split second you are near or when you are rapidly approaching, I feel a fire boiling my blood high within, and at face-to-face contact, the gravitation pull of your bright blue eyes dares the child in me to plunge into the deepest oceans and double dares that same kid to skydive from the highest of skies.

ungodly

as i write
8,000 miles away
there are hunters
in the night sky
who decides
who lives
and dies

in the game
of knucklebones
the rubber ball
is having its attacks
and like picked up jacks
children's bodies meet their axe

who is the one playing God?
who is the one playing Allah?
who is the one with cupped hands?
who is the one claiming victory with these plans?

daydream

When bombs start dropping out of control
and disease struggles to be eradicated,
       what will be the antidote
       for such madness and injustice?
It is at that point we will begin writing
       true life's choreography
       for our children,
       unborn and born crying.
Poems, paintings, songs, and dances
       emerge as cure
       enlightening an unified community.
What will be had is no loyalty to one country
       but loyalty to
              peace
              and
              love
       for the free soul deep within
       all human's state of *Being*.

in my father's silence

Seemly, he's run out of content.
Truth is he's more alive in silence,
        like a war drone falling
        with no congressional consent.

It's been too long,
mistakes from his youth
        sing remorseful song.
He can hear his little boy cry,
        reclaiming pathways of adulterous lie,
        the cancer crack his children live by.

noises become louder and louder

That snapping familiar leash
comes nonstop nightly
        in a hurry, hurried chase.
He must dodge his mother's imagined birds
        left   to   *right*
        jumping *up*
                        and
                                ducking *down.*

Running
and running
down more dirt lanes,
only such heavy clouds
could soften his wings' pains.

episode after episode

Dripped hospital faces looking
    from childhood house
    to his new home,
    like prison cellmate audiences
    standing to his attention.
    The only real affection.

    The only real affection.

be. free. every. time.   *(for my niece)*

be emptied and free
like every time
a mommy and a daddy
choose to give life to a beautiful baby

be emptied and free
like every time
a child
gets back up from falling repeatedly

be emptied and free
like every time
a teenager
inches near depression but picks happy

be emptied and free
like every time
a musician
with few fans finds a stage to sing

be emptied and free
like every time

a dancer
feels rhythm on any floor unconditionally

be emptied and free
like every time
a poet
sits down to write for injustice devotedly

be emptied and free
like every time
a painter
brushes colors for a new world she will see

be emptied and free
like every time
you give every thing inside
for what you *allow* yourself to be

you'll see

Here I am employing metaphor
        like what do I work for?

Power is *not* infinite terror war
        politicking fear for decades more.
Power is the soul of a nation,
        that does *not* destroy
        a soul of another nation.

The poem *you'll see* is in memory of my *tío* (uncle), *Arthur Pina Adame*, who died May 22, 1970 in Cambodia during the Vietnam War. On May 4, 1970, approximately 18 months after Nixon announced a plan to end the war, he wrote to his mom and dad, *"I'm going to make it you'll see."* This was his last letter. Although I was born 16 years after he passed, I vowed to keep his spirit alive. So, *tío* you did make it, because you are a part of what inspires me every day.

keep alive

I see the children
     in anger of a long way down,
head scarcely asking
     for above water.
They scream;

    I want to die!
        or
    I can't breathe!

A holding hug of blood clinched drive
comes with
    confusion,
       blisters from old wood,
    amused,
       consumed
    wishing
       for an ounce of giver good.

I cry,
    they cry
       for the parentless.

And for the innocent part of our infant heart
these children never had,
  you cry,

  Where's my baby?!

  Where's my baby?!

  baby, baby, baby!

I see
obscure chains,
  minivans boarding and bags,
few sweet days melting spring over,
and beautiful adolescent lungs flying
  into thin air summer.
Lunar mists reminded hormonal climbs,
  onto releasing attitude designs,
  like cold mountains
  and their rising *love me!* gases.

I see
feelings of unworthiness lead by
  broken promises

equal to unread fairytales
and soft bed lullabies.

All forcing those inevitable tears
like here's drizzling rain
swiftly becoming
hurricane ripping
clothes, homes, and souls.

What I am trying to say is
I feel less human being,
less inside *myself*,
realizing betrayal's denial,
when another human being
can abuse and rape a child.

Daily, I ask,
in what way can I give myself
to free their self?
to have any part of self that is alive?

I cry,
they cry
for the parentless.

And for the innocent part of our infant heart
these children never had,
    we cry,

       Where's my baby?!

       Where's my baby?!

       baby, baby, baby!

too many

If I were to quote my dream,
I'd be inspired by many,
find a path of those who laugh,
those who growl,
and those who stab
into a quench heart
and its unrecoverable soaking blood.

If I were to bleed my dream,
I'd find the gift of time
enclosed on a caged mime
with an indefinite smile
below several tattooed tears.
I'd find beautiful figure
black dressed in gold stripes
that cover severed skin swipe,
what are decoding lines marked on thighs,
spilling her relentless fears.

They say a dream has to rhyme.
They say a dream has to see.
They say a dream has to be complete.

Well, is a life void not filled
        with inspiration's darkened sleeps,
and is morning's echo not loud enough
        to dry feet from recurrent weeps?

If I were to scream my dream,
she'd let my blood un-bury,
and let its liquid brush stroke
upon every masked mass killer
who denied high spirit flame flurry.
To each roof reuniting a child's sanity with
her innocent clouds and my untainted rain,
together we're flushing out unnatural throat
debris caught in their breathless pain.

If I am my dream,
I'd live by death to save the many,
take back vindictive fingered letters
for those self-inflicting,
to witness children rising,
like an immortal god living,
no longer nailed to drench crosses,
always here forgiving.

tyrant

I am the war you never wanted to reach,
and *here* a drawn sword to save nations,
        from disguised tyrant rulers
        reigning on your heart.

one inked after another

I angered the birds.

I released the channels.

I flooded people down
        their own shallow streams
to save wings hanging
        from tree to tree,
to witness freedom like leaves floating,
        flattened for *godsend.*

As molten rock dust surrounds our sky,
        and upon us now in drought,
influx of river drunks and naked little babies
        who will never be fed.

Their souls like horses jammed in a stable.
My arms can't extent, for they need *yours*.
These burnt blistered hands are incapable.

Here on page is the war for love,
  creating such peace,
  such hunger space left,
  for every unknown innocent dead,
    and
  for compromises needing to be had.

reinterpretation of hunger part I

books
>over

ignorant looks
what spirit whispers
bleeds on pages
inside two realities
life and breath
>over

destruction and death

we march,
>we combat,
>>we uncap

pen for penetration,
>every nation

indefinitely eliminating:
>media controlled mind,
>surveillance team,
>military scheme,
>and empire building

reinterpretation of hunger part II

as our taste intensifies
lips to teeth
we speak one love

we are vibrations
by the billions
sparking new engines

tongues to throats
we sing one peace

we are vibrations
by the billions
sparking new engines

child unknown

Maybe I'm *Jesus'* politics re-captioned,
or never could be poet trapped
in betrayed throat of what isn't heard
from an unknown child's last breath.

Does *God* still dream
       after witnessing
       penitentiary war's
       social class scheme?

Does *He* still wear eternal crown
       when mommies and daddies
       take economic beatings,
       as blood and bone is too thick
       to be wiped from the ground?

Kids will be distracted by play,
       then later tremor
for a deliberate joyful written thought,
       and choose spitting anger
instead of giving vocal talk.

I have seen
sweltering tears on hardwood floor
replace need for an innocent bed,
and distrust of genuine fun,
because rape scars pervade their head.

My children,
your smiles come at a price.
If I don't tell your deepest happiness' secrets,
could I genuinely welcome a hug with love?

One has to be enough.
One too many brain wires like wrists cuffed.
One too many lip scream releases.

> *Can God ask for my forgiveness,*
> *for the work here we re-spark*
> *in avoiding absolute youth lifelessness?*

Would *Jesus* follow *me*,
not die for *me*,
but will *He* hold *your* hand
and observe universal agony
with *you* and *me*?

Would *He* make it?
      Have a *heart* for it?

Or would *He* do all great sacrificing things,
then escape toward premature death,
                      again?

bind

My child and I float
toward the *god of fresh seas,*
hoping forgivers will welcome
the years of tears we cannot cease.

We are *kneeing, begging,*
surrendering infinite refrain
to each night star in constellations,
like they're divine keepers of blueprints for
freeing buried victims of American empires.

What can stop this lightning and rain?
What can shelter cracked vessels like ours
depleted by the currents swallowing pain?
Who will bind some truths
      to acid eroding childhoods
            outside collapsed roof floods?
Who will strap us with life vests,
      fitting as new organs, new knowledge,
         whole hearts,
      to step beyond watered wreckage
         toward *one nation, one message?*

young rose, your woman

Mother called him anything
        but what I am *not* today.
Stillness peeling childish moments
        that taught me every which way.

This temperament embedded
        in a young rose that spilled
to revert color of what my old devil gained.

Actively, black magically,
        he's so quick to love,
            quicker,
        the quickest for let her be gone.

I hate the facts of social rotation,
like the world isn't mature enough
        to end its own demise.
Like an online self-destructive
        human portrait is
        as absolutely filtered
        as hands tickin' clockwise.

I hate the facts of consciousness,
like a patient who disease wept
  for he can *never*
    forget
  anxieties living at his doorstep.
Like erotic events done on *Etch A Sketch,*
  he's rifling to connect
  her dots with one shot left.

  Who gave him this one life?

  which woman?

He's quick to say love fell
into miss I lost control within
  be my friend,
  be my enemy,
  you have to be everything,
    or
  something where
  one fractured chemical well
  here is filled
  by *"oh, this is good enough!"*

she's good enough!

good enough to get to me!

now, letting me into her!

In my I don't care,
         in you're not fair,
there
         planted
                  hallow thoughts
                           and a beautiful stare.

With eyes shut
         and without,
when I touch
those goosebump roots *up*
and *down* your legs, the longing uncovers
what every color petal mirrors,
that liberated woman inside of you,
         a shutter stare true.
Before I have at your fountain
         full of such familiar sweet taste,
like drunk off aged whisky and big cube,

I must blink,
let me not forget to say,

    I
    love
    you.

    Estoy
    enamorado
    de ti.

And hey,
          wait,
do *you feel* like *I feel* when *I* look?
Head to feet,
would *you* one more time?

white line

I hold out my invisible hands,
     zip my mouth,
          point directions,
but everyone witnesses flightless rejections.

When I feel low,
     birds surround below,
     enabled by their imaginations' bow.
As they wait for eyes to meet,
     for arms embrace,
they will chirp our language,
for what else can describe a wanting place,
     with the purest sovereign sunlight
          setting upon your face?

How it makes me collapse
     with unspoken words,
yet leaves my body erect upright and still.

Am I a little too honest too soon?

Where I am kept is reminded,

if my mumble whispers
        could let me break free,
I would leave this solitude immediately!

I see you walk by,
        and I pretend
        to avoid the corner of my eye.
Step by step,
        I glance at the white line,
            left   and   right;
        your curves,
        my misery riding,
            on a road of I want to put
        your happiness first.

How could I abandon these frames?

I need two surrenders,
from you and I, *and* one
promise to fulfill more than wine thirst.

Do you *feel* me every time you smirk?
I'm shaking in response
        to remove this loneliest pride.

serial lover

The way she unclothed
replays photo frame by frame
like joining pavers.
And music isn't playing
but her wanting is like needing
rewind of your favorite 1990s cassette.

As her little diamond heels tap, taps
from apartment front door
to the bed where they slipped off.
Another lens flashes, right before
torture lips latched repeatedly,
and his *for* hers make *one* willingly.

Pelvic spine thrusts against the wall,
influenced by the very second
her smile begins to roar,
and our crime living wave pop
for let's uncork and pour.

We were dangerously evacuated
from misused wine glass open,

what fermented
always came to attention like
        another new creation;
        Fingerprinted conviction,
when we tied each other's ropes,
        suffocated by our own heated arson.

Then, we waited for unwrapped smokes,
and once she let me know the time
        out went my tiny man's giggles.

I held tightly surreal woman on lap,
        whipping and unwinding
            this rolled song map.

There went her brassy coughs
from what had been sucked
mixed with delicate submerged tears;
The remains of what lives
perpetually stuck in our throats,
all initiating memories of angel oxygen coats
        that *drum,*
    drum,
drum for my rhythm born darkness.

my woman hero's stillness

Is it *you* there babe,
who doesn't let these eyelids close alone,
        and let death's fight end here?
Is it in *you* to lay this soul down,
        for never replaced
                but forgiven slightly,
and enable enough landing
        for strangers' wings
which mirror a bed of *you* and *me*?

I shut my lenses,
release my woman hero's stillness,
and a thousand dreams inside fire
        awake imaginary lessons
coming to this actual life precious.

But I'll forever wonder,
where does two people's
        one sound go
whom detach un-alone
but together cannot locate
which vein a kiss can reopen?

this hurt

this hurt
        that I will never tell
is your never knowing
        for where I want to be

this yearn
        fanatically arises
        from poetry scraps
        inside my pockets

for one day,
        just to say,
                i
                like
                you

cheek to cheek, there is a smile in-between
        for what deeply roots
        at each last route of your boots

este dolor   *(Spanish translation for **this hurt**)*

este dolor
     que nunca voy a decir
es que tu nunca vas sabe
     dónde quiero estar

este anhelo
     surge fanáticamente
     a partir trozos de poesía
     dentro de mis bolsillos

por un día,
     sólo para decir,
          me
          gustas

mejilla a mejilla, hay una sonrisa
          entre el medio
     para las raíces profundas
          en cada última ruta
          de sus pasos

mistaken

Tunnel highway voices say poem prevailed
      for long after I am waked,
because in real life, it speaks to you,
      when *you*
don't have anything to reply back,
that can't be found on any app,
      like what is
      too publicly explicit for *Snapchat,*
      and unsearchable with no *hashtag.*

So *here* somehow,
and *there* somewhere,
      children,
whom were *once* self-mutilated,
      now emancipated,
      will see true north blood light
      from orphan black.

To those born blissfully,
To my unborn children,
and *to* those unwanted
      who will patiently start resurrection;

I have sinned with abandoned anger
that was mistaken for pleasure.
I have filled sea sands engrained
by hatefulness that was mistaken for justice.

Is it me who forgets?
>No!
Is it you who has loved so strongly?
>Yes!
We feel both energy sides of *I can't let go.*
And one day,
you will know
all that cases a skeleton
with universal heartbreak
we call,
>I call
>>*forgivable knowledge.*

Are you there with me?
Will you speak from the wire?

If yes,
then these words

have more meaning,
when we are restored wind formations.

so gone

If no,
then I forgive you,
as your chance forgave me enough to sit.

so read on

I will be a drop from the whispering,
     limitless waters,
as you take a cold fountain drink,
      it's me who finds dissolve,
        a calling,
        a freedom,
      defending your bones' fragile worth.

don't you worry

together
     we are here
        endlessly

what doesn't leave me

Who will care that
     my poetry graphic pulse
     is like poor dial-up search engine?
     I am your sweet and lingering,
     with criticism plenty.
     Every one here is
     belonging to moral filtration angle,
     and still, I am the role model
     dancing on rims
     of a pigeonhole's social denial.

I once knew a child
whose first words were,
     "Why are you fluttering your eyes?"

I smiled.

Though her third grade designation,
     she read me,
like a mile before my existence
and way ahead of her peers' persistence.

She was a small version,
pure lion physique,
despite female,
her hair complete
cute mane buoyant.
She cried like a shaky infant
looking for a bottle,
and often laughed,
but when upset,
she did head down *E.T.'s* drunk waddle.

I smiled.

Her eyes wrote;
Who will care that
     my poetry graphic pulse
     is like poor dial-up search engine?
     I am your sweet and lingering,
     with criticism plenty.
     Every one here is
     belonging to moral filtration angle,
     and still, I am the role model
     dancing on rims
     of a pigeonhole's social denial.

People dropped her name with:

neglect

      sex

            reject

                 affect

correct

      protect

            expect

                 respect

She like those words, separated and alone,
      had been CPS system code,
      looking for what is a home.

And each passing day,
I grew closer toward gone
after our last day of school,
      never knowing
who the kid will become,
what lessons will,
or won't be taught.

Today,

> when I read,
> she speaks *through*,
> because all those times
> she would sit
> and read to me.

So tomorrow,

> I will know
> *into* the distance beating,
> there is happiness in a little heart,
> that doesn't leave me.

who loved me

I'm jealous of rain,
for its tiniest diameter rings great beauty,
and though there's an increase here
pounding against window drum,

    I cannot compare.

My heart lives
like a knife
and the way it dices a tomato clear,
a redness so moist annexed by visible seeds.

I rather be inside those clouds,
     obscure and full of luminous powers,
     liberating waters,
     and renew existence on earth.
Maybe, *just maybe* then,
     I could descend
     upon every person who loved me
     with insurmountable gentle worth.

un-alone

Standing at the register
      line for one;
our eternity dismay, lays
like a homeless flower
      catching this plastic bag
          empty composure,
lost in what use to be grown new
      by her days;
He examined roads' reflection miles deep
      behind her sunglass shades
when I demanded our eyes first meet.

I send you best regards
      among story resonances'
      from fumbling two lips,
towards which
      switch
must amend my un-alone words;
      when I can still hear your breaths
         slowly *whispering, linking*
      smoke filled pages with these
      convalescence's intimate concerns.

faster

When her butterfly flutter
dissolved my full air,
in came forensic entries
for what it's like to feel
sudden deaths of
hatchlings' energies.

Orgasming as one,
we struck premonition
like bigger apparatuses'
circles
after road kill seizure;
Eating the fat but
leaving bones and muscles
unknotted
in the only way we know

one last existence.

and faster

My apprehensive desire,
       my precursor,
died in a pure promise box faster
       and faster;
I am sorry loving you
       lasted a little bit longer,
could not be stronger,
       than me giving you
relentless adorned shiver.

my angry sore loser

My more than lil' addictive pleasure,
looks at me like I'm a peasant.
What comes alive there in your mind?
When you say, *"It is your angry sore loser."*
Is it how I remember?
In one coffee shop, then another by patio
and feathers from unplanned lake waterfowl,
when *you* draped
my wet heart in your black hand towel,
        droplet after droplet
like a strawberry dips in chocolate.
But now, am I among slaughter gnats
              who surround that same fruit?

So, I'll cut further *living the deadest sweetness.*
From first time we were chair interlaced for
popcorn and theatre, to a day in picture-
perfect summer, how I rocked you poolside
on your birthday. As lonely stars sheltered
my eyes *into* yours, *we learned to live stranger,*
endured to build temporary homes, and to always
have a place kept there for you to let me treasure.

sensation

Bodies parachute
       but my heart leaps out,
ricocheting off those times *you* had *me*
fully satisfied, caressed without doubt.

Picture after picture,
a *Texas*-sized white blur
surrenders upon
two flames of capital city fire,
my torcher and my heavenly producer;
Our climax inches close to sinister;
       I imbricate immeasurable *her,*
           roll over,
           smiles *there* undercover
       toward umpteenth *goodnight lover.*

When my nose is the coldest,
I come across her long jacket
       and my hollow chest,
a repetitive mystery
       for what she would heal next;
With her inducing pretty red cheeks,

lit I became
as maniac barefoot dance went,
'til we finally let our worry rest.

How she makes me break
and stitches soul back to life again,
like laceration regeneration.

She suspends me so constant
      at any given moment,
like reason for an ashtray kept,
table placed ready
for blackest residue on its brim;
On the other end,
lips fuse symbolic go
for slow explosive thoughts
      arousing wires in this brain
and deep chambers the same.

How she secures
      heart-detonation
           foundation
with first kiss touch,
my most needed sensation.

art cure

is poetry deliberately written
>*for love obsessed*
>*endless acceptance*
>*by a childish charm*
>*begging for attention?*
or is this an endless street drainage
>*ocean sinking adulterer*
>*and alcohol by accident?*

I've observed
early family heartache's
self-possessed demon ghosts
>brought to this life,
which could *not* filter any contaminant.

What is left,
>*I think,*
is passion patterns remote controlled
vexing for location of trust and respect.

I think
the hardest part

is being unconditionally still
and receiving so much affection
in a soothing silence,
like vaccine without injection.

And the easiest thing
is giving it to a woman,
      un-claimable,
in most times as untitled work,
      art cure
      of all that is dying and living,
      equally.

I am not a child under spell conceiving.
I am a changing.
I am a sunset waiting.
I am a coastline content,
      staring
at a million pictures
      that feature *love's harmony*
as true blood irresistible adoption;
      a new discovery of myself
      because each person
      gave me free shore passage

onto first footsteps of their ocean.
I am permanently indebted
for their one-by-one baptism.
It is this man's admission,
God to woman,
needed time and time again.

stingy chemical man

my religion
> is every thing I have touched
>> *since the alarm went off*

my religion
> is what I haven't put my hands on
>> *since the alarm went off*

I'm not a perfect preacher
I'm not a frequent sinner

we are not
we are not

I'm a stingy chemical man
> who hasn't fallen out of love
> with the first time
> medicated by every time

oh, how her ease
> will free
>> *me*
> into what we are made for

this is why
I can hide my trembling
until
she comes home once more

wings may crash

it is as if you grab a propeller
  fly,
    empower,
  then lower,
    skydive,
  straight down,
    walk
  into the same moving propeller

pieces,
  pieces,
    pieces

for *you*,
  I
  am
  pieces

who am I to never suffer?

who am I to find truth in a dreamer?

inside an instance,

who am I to be put back together?

I imagine
a thousand more lives to have again
this one moment
yet, I'm okay with death
because unmistaken passion found

for *you,*

I

am

not

broken

as I am

I think I have lost people in these poems.
I think I love to be un-alone.
I think I discover ghosts in my solitary zones.
I think I could never leave it all alone.

I think I think too much.
I think I should have eaten lunch.
I think I need a woman's touch.
I think I should've had the date gone Dutch.

I think of the child I have not had.
I think of the children beloved
by their grandparents
but cannot depend on a mom or dad.
I think of being an educator
and what I can add.
I think of those compassionate spirits
making this world a little less mad.

coming back to San Antonio

My grandma Aurora was born in *Nuevo León*.
She made the best American sandwiches,
but her specialty was *menudo* on holidays.
My other grandparents Sulema and Anselmo
were the closest couple to perfection.
However, when they dated,
they would sit at the back
away from a mostly white section.
What they told me as a kid,
English could only be talked
near the restaurant front door,
and if they spoke Spanish,
that is what the back is for.

Yes, my parents grew up
in a Spanish speaking household,
but they only taught us English.
Routinely in college, I learned how
frustrating race can be and what could
or could not have been done different.
To this day, people will question
who I am and *what I wasn't*.

growing

when I was younger,
I danced *cumbias* like *Selena,* shook my knees
with *Elvis'* and *Michael Jackson's* energy
I pretended to rap like *Tupac,*
sing sweet taboo like *Sade's* R&B
I recited speeches from *Chavez, Dr. King,*
and each *Kennedy*
I wanted to be *David Robinson*
to bring home championship rings
I wished to be all things

when I was younger,
I wondered when mom would come home
after arguing again with my father
I cried for my brother
to include me with his friends
I looked forward to my grandma speaking
the Spanish rosary on weekends

when I was younger,
after my best ball game,
my father

yelled at me to be better
I questioned if his army helicopter accident
and its *PTSD* anxiety played a factor
I prayed one day *Vietnam*
would somehow bring home his brother
I believed losing his dad too soon
didn't make him more sensitive
one problem to another
I wondered if it caused him
to cheat on my mother
I give thanks to the Chilean girl
who taught me I couldn't be a victim
for someone else's life any longer

When I grew up,
I became appreciative
for having a family.
I found new passions
and great people inside my apathy.
I took pride in being *Tejano*
and a graduate of once segregated *UT*.
I felt blessed for serving
and seeking
change in a community.

When I grew up,
I searched harder for truth after *9/11*.
I relied on pen and peace
to eliminate fear as a political weapon.
I admired my new best friend who is *Muslim*.
I learned continually to welcome non-violent
answers from any color, any faith,
any language, and any country custom.

breathing

Here I am with limited recipe,
trying to feed the only man
who has ever loved me.
I look at my dad
extremely skinny
from his incapability to want to eat,
and I barely utter a word out in real life.
I try to make amends talking in my mind.

When I came to the thought
that he could die,
I couldn't stop thinking
one day death will find me,
and I would no longer be breathing.
I love breathing,
but we take its giving for granted.

We take *and we take*
as if humans are immortal;
We fight *and we fight*
to occupy space
stripping atmospheres for survival.

Can we rest in this moment
and ask,
does the air ever say,
don't you dare breathe into us?
So how can we demand to *God*
what not to take from us?

when a good thing isn't so bad

In one touch,
I needed you to trust
the next touch and a last
would mean the same,
     every time
we undressed our animal within us,
that could not restrain its tame.
My touch
is *not* a sex game.
My touch
is *not* someone's body I needed to claim.
My touch is every thing in *me*
you made feel un-invisible,
simple.

Healing again
and again,
I do not have shame.

I came to the understanding
     I am
     We are treasured poets

when I surrender my flesh to you
inside our purest moments,
when I give up my tongue to you
by the smallest dosages.

I learned I was born to adore her,
then,
I learned I am the angriest sore loser,
but she taught me I can be good
at caring for someone else's children,
and she taught me I can be good
at loving somebody's inner woman.

her mind's spirit *(for ila)*

A hundred or so stringed balloons,
in many colors over celebration city,
went off inside her mind freely,
when we were hours at a time on the phone.

This was her thought process,
for each string
her tender hands snatched
had been a blessing.
What went off was
an idea of her and me,
or her dreams only,
maybe career objective,
life's uncertainty,
and any thing needing to be
worked on wholeheartedly.

intensely me

As annoying as I am me,
I will always know what it means
  to be *that guy,*
a parasite blood hunter,
like a mosquito in the night
  who flies unnoticed
piercing skin, lover *after* lover.

As sensitive as I am me,
I will always know what it means
  to be intensely me,
a castaway poet
with no umbrella on bended knees
praying for sunrise showers,
  who rhymes absurd
as much as it pours,
just to tell you how much I miss *yours.*

heart exit

I don't know if my heart will always beat
childishly like book cuts of *The Giving Tree*,
or if I honestly expose to the teeth what's
hidden in every grown man's skeleton closet.
Perhaps, I could be hanging on to
      too much silence,
somewhere between drain and a drop,
      like what's leaking
in a *New York* borough apartment faucet.
I may never know
      who's thirsty enough for it,
but for keepsakes, here's
      what is real for you
      in my unseen chest locket:

us locking hands, *me* pinning *you* down,
fears coming out *while* colorful mysterious
      light starts its dangle down
how feelings come as fast as sprayed perfume
in thin air with a smell this fresh
how I won't forget the rarest vibration
your empathy chills gave against this flesh

every wall I turn to,
     the exit no different,
has
     you
in highway tunnels of climaxing petal chime
like beauty arch wisteria and rose mallow
                 leaves
                 vine